Algrove Publishing Limited
36 Mill Street, P.O. Box 1238
Almonte, Ontario, Canada K0A 1A0

Telephone: (613) 256-0350
Fax: (613) 256-0360
Email: sales@algrove.com

Library and Archives Canada Cataloguing in Publication

Ahern, Gene
    Our boarding house with major hoople, 1927 / Gene Ahern.

(Classic reprint series)
Cartoons.
ISBN 1-897030-34-7

1. American wit and humor, Pictorial. 2. Boardinghouses-
Caricatures and cartoons. I. Title. II. Series: Classic reprint series
(Almonte, Ont.)
PN6728.O86A44 2005   741.5'973   C2005-904757-7

Printed in Canada
#1-8-05

Publisher's Note

When publishing any material as old as this, there is a haunting suspicion that maybe all the lovers of the old cartoons have gone the way of the old cartoons. We live in hope that this is not so. Publishing of years after 1927 will depend on the response of aging readers to this first volume.

Leonard G. Lee, Publisher
Almonte, Ontario
August 2005

How We Make Our Books - *You may not have noticed, but this book is quite different from other softcover books you might own. The vast majority of paperbacks, whether mass-market or the more expensive trade paperbacks, have the pages sheared and notched at the spine so that they may be glued together. The paper itself is often of newsprint quality. Over time, the paper will brown and the spine will crack if flexed. Eventually the pages fall out.*

All of our softcover books, like our hardcover books, have sewn bindings. The pages are sewn in signatures of sixteen or thirty-two pages and these signatures are then sewn to each other. They are also glued at the back but the glue is used primarily to hold the cover on, not to hold the pages together.

We also use only acid-free paper in our books. This paper does not yellow over time. A century from now, this book will have paper of its original color and an intact binding, unless it has been exposed to fire, water, or other catastrophe.

There is one more thing you will note about this book as you read it; it opens easily and does not require constant hand pressure to keep it open. In all but the smallest sizes, our books will also lie open on a table, something that a book bound only with glue will never do unless you have broken its spine.

The cost of these extras is well below their value and while we do not expect a medal for incorporating them, we did want you to notice them.

OUR BOARDING HOUSE

with

Major Hoople

GENE AHERN.

1927

Algrove Publishing
Classic Reprint Series

THE SUIT IS IN DRY-DOCK

PUTTING OIL ON THE FIRE

THEY FAIL TO IMPRESS JAKE

THE SPELLING BEE

FIGURING OUT THE "SQUARE" FOR HIMSELF —

JAKE SQUARES HIMSELF

THE MAJOR'S PALS ARRIVE

THE CURTAIN ON THEIR VACATION

GENE AHERN.

THE BIG
SURPRISE PARTY TOMORROW

If you like this book you may be interested our Classic Reprints
by the other great cartoonist of the last century, J.R. Williams.

Out Our Way
20s, 30s, 40s

Classic Cowboy Cartoons

U.S. Cavalry Cartoons

The Bull of the Woods

Publications by Algrove Publishing Limited

The following is a list of titles from our popular *"Classic Reprint Series"*
as well as other publications by Algrove Publishing Limited.

ARCHITECTURE, BUILDING, AND DESIGN

Item #	Title
49L8038	☐ A BOOK OF ALPHABETS WITH PLAIN, ORNAMENTAL, ANCIENT AND MEDIAEVAL STYLES
49L8096	☐ A GLOSSARY OF TERMS USED IN ENGLISH ARCHITECTURE
49L8016	☐ BARN PLANS & OUTBUILDINGS
49L8046	☐ BEAUTIFYING THE HOME GROUNDS
49L8112	☐ BUILDING WITH LOGS AND LOG CABIN CONSTRUCTION
49L8092	☐ DETAIL, COTTAGE AND CONSTRUCTIVE ARCHITECTURE
49L8015	☐ FENCES, GATES & BRIDGES
49L8706	☐ FROM LOG TO LOG HOUSE
49L0720	☐ HOMES & INTERIORS OF THE 1920'S
49L8111	☐ LOW-COST WOOD HOMES
49L8030	☐ SHELTERS, SHACKS & SHANTIES
49L8050	☐ STRONG'S BOOK OF DESIGNS
49L8064	☐ THE ARCHITECTURE OF COUNTRY HOUSES
49L8021	☐ THE INTERNATIONAL CYCLOPEDIA OF MONOGRAMS
49L8023	☐ THE OPEN TIMBER ROOFS OF THE MIDDLE AGES

CLASSIC CATALOGS

Item #	Title
49L8004	☐ BOULTON & PAUL, LTD. 1898 CATALOGUE
49L8098	☐ CATALOG OF MISSION FURNITURE 1913 – *COME-PACKT FURNITURE*
49L8097	☐ MASSEY-HARRIS CIRCA 1914 CATALOG
49L8089	☐ OVERSHOT WATER WHEELS FOR SMALL STREAMS
49L8079	☐ WILLIAM BULLOCK & CO. – *HARDWARE CATALOG CIRCA 1850*

GARDENING

Item #	Title
49L8082	☐ CANADIAN WILD FLOWERS (C. P. TRAILL)
49L8113	☐ COLLECTING SEEDS OF WILD PLANTS AND SHIPPING LIVE PLANT MATERIAL
49L8029	☐ FARM WEEDS OF CANADA
49L8056	☐ FLORA'S LEXICON
49L8705	☐ REFLECTIONS ON THE FUNGALOIDS
49L8076	☐ THE WILDFLOWERS OF AMERICA
49L8057	☐ THE WILDFLOWERS OF CANADA

HUMOR AND PUZZLES

Item #	Title
49L8074	☐ ARE YOU A GENIUS? WHAT IS YOUR I.Q?
49L8106	☐ CLASSIC COWBOY CARTOONS, VOL. 1
49L8109	☐ CLASSIC COWBOY CARTOONS, VOL. 2
49L8118	☐ CLASSIC COWBOY CARTOONS, VOL. 3
49L8119	☐ CLASSIC COWBOY CARTOONS, VOL. 4
49L8072	☐ CLASSIC PUZZLES AND HOW TO SOLVE THEM
49L8103	☐ GRANDMOTHER'S PUZZLE BOOK
49L8081	☐ MR. PUNCH WITH ROD AND GUN – *THE HUMOUR OF FISHING AND SHOOTING*
49L8073	☐ NAME IT! THE PICTORIAL QUIZ BOOK
49L8126	☐ OUR BOARDING HOUSE WITH MAJOR HOOPLE – *1927*
49L8125	☐ OUT OUR WAY – *SAMPLER 20s, 30s & 40s*
49L8044	☐ SAM LOYD'S PICTURE PUZZLES
49L8071	☐ THE BULL OF THE WOODS, VOL. 1
49L8080	☐ THE BULL OF THE WOODS, VOL. 2
49L8104	☐ THE BULL OF THE WOODS, VOL. 3
49L8114	☐ THE BULL OF THE WOODS, VOL. 4
49L8115	☐ THE BULL OF THE WOODS, VOL. 5
49L8116	☐ THE BULL OF THE WOODS, VOL. 6
49L8084	☐ THE ART OF ARTHUR WATTS
49L8107	☐ U.S. CAVALRY CARTOONS

NAVAL AND MARINE

Item #	Title
49L8090	☐ BOAT-BUILDING AND BOATING
49L8707	☐ BUILDING THE NORWEGIAN SAILING PRAM *(MANUAL AND PLANS)*
49L8708	☐ BUILDING THE SEA URCHIN *(MANUAL AND PLANS)*
49L8078	☐ MANUAL OF SEAMANSHIP FOR BOYS AND SEAMEN OF THE ROYAL NAVY, 1904
49L8095	☐ SAILING SHIPS AT A GLANCE
49L8099	☐ THE SAILOR'S WORD-BOOK
49L8058	☐ THE YANKEE WHALER
49L8025	☐ THE YOUNG SEA OFFICER'S SHEET ANCHOR
49L8061	☐ TRADITIONS OF THE NAVY

REFERENCE

Item #	Title
49L8083	☐ AMERICAN MECHANICAL DICTIONARY – KNIGHT VOL. I, VOL. II, VOL. III
49L8093	☐ 507 MECHANICAL MOVEMENTS
49L8024	☐ 1800 MECHANICAL MOVEMENTS AND DEVICES
49L8055	☐ 970 MECHANICAL APPLIANCES AND NOVELTIES OF CONSTRUCTION
49L8602	☐ ALL THE KNOTS YOU NEED
49L8077	☐ CAMP COOKERY
49L8001	☐ LEE'S PRICELESS RECIPES
49L8018	☐ THE BOY'S BOOK OF MECHANICAL MODELS
49L8019	☐ WINDMILLS AND WIND MOTORS

TRADES

Item #	Title
49L8014	☐ BOOK OF TRADES
49L8086	☐ FARM BLACKSMITHING
49L8031	☐ FARM MECHANICS
49L8087	☐ FORGING
49L8027	☐ HANDY FARM DEVICES AND HOW TO MAKE THEM
49L8002	☐ HOW TO PAINT SIGNS & SHO' CARDS
49L8054	☐ HOW TO USE THE STEEL SQUARE
49L8094	☐ THE YOUNG MILL-WRIGHT AND MILLER'S GUIDE
49L8053	☐ THE METALWORKING LATHE

WOODWORKING AND CRAFTS

Item #	Title
49L8101	☐ ARTS-CRAFTS LAMPS & SHADES – *HOW TO MAKE THEM*
49L8012	☐ BOY CRAFT
49L8110	☐ CHAIN SAW AND CROSSCUT SAW TRAINING COURSE
49L8048	☐ CLAY MODELLING AND PLASTER CASTING
49L8005	☐ COLONIAL FURNITURE
49L8065	☐ COPING SAW WORK
49L8032	☐ DECORATIVE CARVING, PYROGRAPHY AND FLEMISH CARVING
49L8091	☐ FURNITURE DESIGNING AND DRAUGHTING
49L8049	☐ HANDBOOK OF TURNING
49L8020	☐ MISSION FURNITURE, HOW TO MAKE IT
49L8033	☐ ORNAMENTAL AND DECORATIVE WOOD CARVINGS
49L8059	☐ PROJECTS FOR WOODWORK TRAINING
49L8003	☐ RUSTIC CARPENTRY
49L8085	☐ SKELETON LEAVES AND PHANTOM FLOWERS
49L8068	☐ SPECIALIZED JOINERY
49L8052	☐ STANLEY COMBINATION PLANES –*THE 45, THE 50 & THE 55*
49L8034	☐ THE ART OF WHITTLING
49L8047	☐ TIMBER – *FROM THE FOREST TO ITS USE IN COMMERCE*
49L8042	☐ TURNING FOR AMATEURS
49L8039	☐ VIOLIN MAKING AS IT WAS, AND IS
49L8013	☐ YOU CAN MAKE IT
49L8035	☐ YOU CAN MAKE IT FOR CAMP & COTTAGE
49L8036	☐ YOU CAN MAKE IT FOR PROFIT
49L8067	☐ WOOD HANDBOOK – *WOOD AS AN ENGINEERING MATERIAL*
49L8060	☐ WOODEN PLANES AND HOW TO MAKE THEM

Algrove Publishing Limited, 36 Mill Street, P.O. Box 1238, Almonte, Ontario, Canada K0A 1A0
Telephone: (613) 256-0350   Fax: (613) 256-0360   Email: sales@algrove.com